TEXAS

MALLARD PRESS

Photography
FPG
Odyssey Publishing Ltd

Photo Editor
Annette Lerner

MALLARD PRESS

An imprint of BDD Promotional
Book Company Inc.,
666 Fifth Avenue, New York,
NY 10103

Mallard Press and its
accompanying design and logo
are trademarks of BDD
Promotional Book Company, Inc.

Color separations by Advance
Laser Graphic Arts, Hong Kong.

Printed and bound
in Hong Kong.

ISBN 0-7924-5483-9

*Previous pages: Alamo Chapel,
Mission San Antonio de Valero,
on the San Antonio River, and
(right) Lake Livingstone on the
edge of the Sam Houston
National Forest, East Texas.*

The list of heroes whose names loom large in the history of Texas would probably fill the Pecos 'phone book. But the one Texans honor nearly every day is a woman who has no towns named for her and whose name is nearly forgotten.

Jane Wilkinson Long is considered to be the first English-speaking woman to settle in Texas, which in itself would assure her of a place in its history. But her claim to fame is much greater than that. She arrived in Nacogdoches in 1820 with her husband, Dr. James Long, and a force of volunteers to liberate Texas from the Mexicans after the American Government had agreed to leave it under Spanish control in return for Florida. Long's little army gained a foothold easily, but he knew he would need help if he intended to keep it. With that in mind, he headed for Galveston to enlist the services of the pirate Jean Lafitte and his men. While he was gone, the Mexicans counterattacked and Jane was among the people who escaped into Louisiana where she was eventually reunited with her husband.

Long was no quitter and soon he and his wife and their two daughters were on their way back to Texas. After building a fort he moved on again, this time to Mexico City to try his hand at negotiation. His family stayed behind in the fort with a little band of volunteer soldiers.

Long had not gone far when he was tossed into a Mexican prison. When word got back to the fort, the volunteers took off, leaving Jane alone with her children, a teenage black slave named Kian and a dog named Galveston. The deserters took most of the food with them, but they left behind a collection of fishhooks and a rusty old cannon.

The women, children and dog survived winter in the fort, living on oysters and fish and raw courage. Then one day, a band of Indians appeared outside the walls. Jane was certain it was to be her last day on earth.

She decided not to go without a fight. After hoisting a red petticoat to the top of the flagpole, she fired a blast from the cannon in the general direction of the approaching red men. The cannon ball didn't hit any of them, but it made them stop and think, and after a short pow wow, they turned and ran.

A few weeks later, the twenty-one-year-old Mrs. Long gave birth to her third daughter. The child was an orphan. Her father had been shot by the Mexicans. "An accident," they said.

When Jane discovered that her husband had been killed, she rode off in the direction of Mexico City to see to it that his killer was punished. However, before reaching her destination, she decided that she was on a fool's errand, turned around and headed back home to Mississippi. But she didn't stay long. Even then, the lure of Texas was powerful. Even though she had been raised in Mississippi, Texas had become her home. So a few years later she went back and settled down there, the very model of the ideal Texas woman.

Jane Wilkinson Long was not an unusual Texas woman. On the contrary, she is fairly typical of the thousands who followed her and inspired their husbands, their children and others like themselves to civilize this wild land. It isn't known why she chose to raise a flannel petticoat over the fort to scare off the Indians that day, because she had something much better. It was something powerful enough to scare off armies of men with ideas of taking on the Texans.

Before she left for Nacogdoches, she and her sister had designed and sewn a flag for her husband's volunteer army. It was made of white silk with a red stripe and red fringe all around. And in a blue field to the left, it had a white star. A lone star.

Jane Long's star still hangs high over Texas from the streets of Laredo to the Red River Valley, from the Rio Grande's citrus groves to San Antonio's Alamo, from the grasslands of the Panhandle to the wide open spaces west of the Pecos. It is the tie that binds Texans together. Perhaps, somehow, Jane must have known it would.

Above: Dallas Alley, West End Historic District, Dallas (these pages). Left: the Infomart Building, and (facing page) the Reunion Complex and Dallas by night. The Infomart Building stands in the Dallas Market Center World Trade Center on Stemmons Freeway. Almost every well-known computer company based in the States has rented space in the Infomart Building. It was designed by Martin Growald to imitate London's Crystal Palace.

Left: the eighty-foot-tall flagpoles outside Dallas City Hall, designed by I.M. Pei, and (below) the Dallas skyline from Municipal Plaza. The stark modernity of the City Hall shows how far Dallas has come from the days in 1841 when John Neely Bryan built his cabin in the area on the banks of the Trinity River. It is thought that the subsequent development was named for vice president (1845-49) George Mifflin Dallas. The wealth of Dallas was created first by cotton and then oil.

Facing page: Aldredge House, Swiss Avenue, and (right) Thanksgiving Square, both in Dallas. The spiral building in the background is the Chapel of Thanksgiving. Aldredge House, built in 1916, is now part of the Swiss Avenue Historic Association. The Swiss Avenue area is the site of over 200 magnificent homes in a variety of architectural styles.

Left: the War Memorial and Convention Center, Dallas (these pages). Below: the Infomart Building in the Dallas Market Center World Trade Center, incorporating 10 million square feet, housing clothing, computer, toy and furniture retailers. Facing page: the Dallas skyline reaching ever upward. Henry Cobb of I.M. Pei & Partners described the design and construction of his gray, pointed 1986 First Interstate Tower (initially the Allied Bank) to the left of the picture as "geometry pursued with rigor."

Above: the prominent dome-topped tower of the Reunion Complex. Its geodesic globe contains a revolving restaurant. The Reunion Complex has no connection with the abandoned socialist colony of that name. In fact, one of the backers of the Complex project was the son of billionaire anti-socialist propagandist H.L. Hunt. Right: the Dallas skyline.

Facing page: (top) Southfork Ranch, featured in the television soap opera Dallas, and (bottom) Main Street, Fort Worth, looking North, with the Lone Star of Texas marked out in contrasting brickwork at its center. Right: Main Street festively lit up for Christmas. At its head stands Tarrant County Courthouse.

A mural of cattle painted vividly on the red granite wall of a building below the new City Hall in Fort Worth. Oil only replaced cattle as Fort Worth's main industry in 1912. Between 1866-84 over 10 million head of cattle passed through Fort Worth, alias "Cowtown," following the Chisholm Trail.

Left: cypress trees hung with Spanish moss in Caddo Lake, Caddo Lake State Park, near Jefferson. Facing page: Old Fort Parker Historic Site near Groesbeck. Here, in 1834, John Parker built his fort. Two years later Commanche attacked it, capturing five members of the Parker family, one of whom, Cynthia Ann, lived as a Commanche for many years before being returned to her Texan relatives. She died pining for her lost Indian freedom aged thirty-seven years.

Above: the skyline of Houston behind the low building housing the Albert Thomas Space Hall of Fame. The gable-roofed skyscraper beyond houses the Republic Bank, designed by Philip Johnson to imitate the look of early banking houses in Antwerp. Left: the 570-foot-high San Jacinto Monument in San Jacinto Battleground Park, near Houston. The monument commemorates Sam Houston's victory over the Mexican general, Santa Anna, at the Battle of San Jacinto in 1836. The monument is sinking under its own weight. Facing page: the Wortham Fountains in Tranquility Park, downtown Houston.

Facing page: Houston at night, and (right) the Strand, Galveston. Houston was the result of the vision of two New York real estate promoters, J.K. and A.C. Allen, who were looking for a suitable site for a "great center of government and commerce." Galveston's Strand is also known as the Wall Street of the Southwest and is incorporated in the Strand Historic District, created to protect antebellum landmark buildings.

Right: University of Texas Tower and the Littlefield Memorial Fountain, sculpted by Pompeo Coppini, Austin. The University opened on College Hill in 1883, forty-four years after the state created the University of Texas. The cost of two wars delayed its completion. Below: Town Lake, Austin. Facing page: Texas State Capitol Building, Austin, completed in 1888. The Capitol's cornerstone was laid on the forty-ninth anniversary of the Battle of San Jacinto, March 2, 1885, to a forty-nine gun salute. The bronze monument in front of it, dedicated to Terry's Texas Rangers, was also sculpted by Pompeo Coppini, and was mounted in 1907 to commemorate the Texas Rangers who served the Confederacy during the Civil War.

Facing page top: the ranch house, known as the "Texas White House," at Lyndon B. Johnson Ranch, now part of the Lyndon B. Johnson Historical Park. Johnson said of this area: "It is impossible to live on this land without being a part of it." Facing page bottom: Arneson Theater, San Antonio, on the Paseo del Rio, or River Walk, at the entrance to La Villita, or the Little Town. Right: the 1873 Gothic-Revival Cathedral at 115 Main Plaza, San Antonio, designed by François Giraud.

Corpus Christi Marina, enclosed within a protective breakwater. The Port of Corpus Christi was established in 1926, and is the deepest port on the Gulf coast.

Facing page and left: Mission San José y San Miguel de Aguayo, built between 1768-82, was the second mission to be built on the San Antonio River. It is one of the finest to be preserved in San Antonio Missions National Historical Park. Its much acclaimed Rosa Window was sculpted by Pedro Huizar, and is said to have been named for the woman he loved who was lost at sea on her way to join him at the mission. The mission was founded by one of the most energetic missionaries of that time, Antonio Margil de Jesús. Above: the Botanical Garden in San Antonio.

Above: the Window, seen from the Basin in Big Bend National Park. Big Bend is Texas' largest park, covering more than 700,000 acres. Left: Fulton Mansion, Fulton, was built by Colonel George Ware Fulton, a cattle baron, and completed in 1876. Robert E. Lee and Jefferson Davis were guests here. Facing page: the Rio Grande in Big Bend National Park.

Left: the barren, 2,000-feet-tall peak of El Capitan in Guadalupe Mountains National Park (below). Facing page: ice-covered vegetation under fog in Chisos Basin, Big Bend National Park. The beauty of this now protected land was remarked upon by Mary Austin Holley as early as 1836: "Quite unexpectedly, a report has reached the public ear that the country lying west of the Sabine River is a tract of surpassing beauty, exceeding even our best western lands in productiveness, and with a climate perfectly salubrious, and of a temperature, at all seasons of the year, most delightful."

Cattle ranching in Texas. The heyday of Texan cattle ranching was from the mid-1860s to the 1880s. Later the profitability of cattle was outdone by that of oil.

Left: morning breaks over Hunt County, eastern Texas. Facing page: Inks Lake in Inks Lake State Park in Texas' Hill Country. There are six lakes in this area off the lower Colorado River.

Facing page: Presidio County, and (right) Enchanted Rock State Natural Area, in Central Texas. Enchanted Rock, eighteen miles north of Fredericksburg, is a billion-year-old granite mountain – at the center of many Indian ghost stories and travelers' tales. Below: Palo Duro Canyon, twenty miles south of Amarillo. Geologists believe that this spectacular chasm was sculpted over 90 million years ago by wind and water erosion. This multi-colored canyon is 120 miles long and up to two miles wide in places, its walls often reaching 1,120 feet in height. Spanish explorer Francisco Vásquez de Coronado came across the canyon in 1541. Palo Duro is Spanish for "hard wood," referring to the juniper trees found around it.

Right: cornfields in Central Texas, and (overleaf) the towers of downtown Houston.